Shakespeare
and His Theatre

John Russell Brown
Illustrated by David Gentleman

Lothrop, Lee & Shepard Books
New York

Text copyright © 1982 by John Russell Brown
Illustrations copyright © 1982 by David Gentleman
First published in Great Britain in 1982 by Kestrel Books

Printed in Great Britain
First U.S. Edition
1 2 3 4 5 6 7 8 9 10

LIBRARY OF CONGRESS CATALOGING IN PUBLICATION DATA
Brown, John Russell. Shakespeare and His Theatre.

   Summary: Describes what we now believe Shakespeare's Globe
Theatre was like, who the people were who ran it and how they
worked, and what Shakespeare's plays were like in performance, as
he saw them.
   1. Globe Theatre (Southwark, London, England) – Juvenile
literature. 2. Shakespeare, William, 1564-1616 – Stage history – To
1625 – Juvenile literature. 3. Theater – England – London – History –
16th century – Juvenile literature. 4. Theater – England – London –
History – 17th century – Juvenile literature.
[1. Globe Theatre (Southwark, London, England). 2. Shakespeare,
William, 1564-1616 – Stage history – To 1625. 3. Theater – England –
History] I. Gentleman, David, ill. II. Title.
PR2920.B7   792'.09421'64   81-8441
ISBN 0-688-00850-X   AACR2

Contents

Introduction

No stick, stone or brick of Shakespeare's theatre survived the Great Fire of London in 1666. And no one, before then, had ever sat down in the auditorium to draw a picture of what the inside of that theatre was like. One rough sketch with a few characters standing in a row is all the pictorial evidence we have suggesting what actors looked like during an original performance of one of Shakespeare's plays.

What has survived, more than this, is a very crude drawing of the interior of another theatre that Shakespeare must have visited and several very, very small pictures of the outside of Shakespeare's theatre; together with a number of documents such as wills, evidence for law cases, a builder's contract, account books, city regulations, actors' manuscripts, and so forth. There are also the texts of plays performed at that time, some references in published books, and notes in diaries, letters and the margins of other documents.

All the evidence is fragmentary and some of it contradictory. Scholars have worked over every scrap for many years, checking their findings, testing them in models and working drawings, consulting architects, builders, actors, stage technicians and each other. Long and detailed debates have been published in learned journals, not always without angry words. But now the dust of argument seems to be settling and general agreement has been reached on many of the problems of reconstruction.

This book tries to *show* the result of all the scholars' work. It describes what we now believe Shakespeare's theatre was like and invites you to look at what was inside its walls and behind its stage. It introduces you to the people who ran the theatre, and gives some idea of how they worked. It should help you to imagine what Shakespeare's plays were like in performance, as he saw them.

How the Theatre was Built

The theatre in which all Shakespeare's greatest plays were performed was called the Globe. The word 'globe' had entered the English language less than fifty years earlier to refer to spherical models of the world that was being newly discovered. As the name for a playhouse it made bold claims.

With the theatre's name went a painted sign which showed great Hercules, as a strong man, holding the round world upon his shoulders. We often see pubs today with signs illustrating the King's Head, Red Bull or Blue Lion. In Shakespeare's day, when many people could neither read nor write, such signs were absolutely necessary for identification: taverns, shops, some private houses, workshops and ships all had them. Crests or badges worn by soldiers in battle fulfilled the same purpose. Like a trade-mark, Hercules and his globe announced: 'Here you can see a whole world supported by our efforts.' The theatre also had a Latin motto: '*Totus mundis agit historiem*' – which put the picture's announcement into words for learned passers-by.

Built in 1599, during the last years of the reign of Elizabeth I, the Globe was one of the first playhouses to open in London. Previously, actors had been homeless. They had travelled around the country, performing in the halls of great houses and colleges, and on portable platforms, or 'scaffolds', set up in public buildings or crowded inn-yards. Shakespeare, as a boy, would have seen plays performed in this way. But when he was twelve years old and still a schoolboy in Stratford-upon-Avon, the first permanent theatre was built in London and called, quite simply, The Theatre. James Burbage was the man responsible. He leased a site just outside the Bishopsgate entrance to the City of London and began building in 1576.

Burbage was a fast worker and knew how to take risks. He opened his theatre before it was properly finished, so that the early profits could pay for completing and furnishing the building. It was in use by the summer of 1577, the year in which Francis Drake set out to be the first man to sail round the world from West to East. Both Burbage and Drake encouraged others to follow them. Merchant Venturers explored new territories and the very next year a second theatre, the Curtain, was in operation. By 1587 and 1595, the Rose and the Swan, both south of the River Thames, had had their first performances.

By the end of the century the great Spanish Armada had been beaten back from the shores of England and many Elizabethans were planning to settle in the newly discovered colonies and so enjoy fabulous riches and a new, adventurous life. When Burbage's first theatre had to be replaced in 1599, it was called the Globe. Its future was identified with adventurers sailing round the world in search of great riches and new marvels.

The halls and inn-yards in which actors had previously performed were square or rectangular, but the Globe, like some other early theatres, was a circular, wooden building. This form suited the theatre's name and made the building highly distinctive. In the history-play of *Henry the Fifth*, written for the Globe, Shakespeare called the theatre a 'Wooden O'.

Its round shape, together with the height of its three tall storeys, made the Globe a landmark for miles around. Neighbouring buildings were long, narrow and comparatively low, as was most convenient for their timber-frame construction. The numerous roof-lines followed the streets or were close together at right angles to them. The only other buildings at all like theatres were the arenas used for displays of bull- and bear-baiting.

As a visitor emerged from the riverside streets on the south bank of the Thames, the Globe Theatre, and a neighbouring bear-baiting arena, caught the eye at once. It would be clearly visible, too, above the roof-tops, as a playgoer waited for a boat to ferry him over the river from the more crowded city to the north.

A circular building about one hundred feet (or thirty metres) across could not be constructed simply out of the comparatively short timber beams which were the standard structural materials of the times. The builders had to go to great trouble to achieve a twenty-or twenty-four-sided frame for the Globe, with angled joints and three galleries supported with many pillars. They did so in order that audiences could see and hear a play as clearly as possible. They were also aware – and proud of the fact – that they were copying the huge amphitheatres of Ancient Rome, that had been used for public spectacles and gladiatorial combats. The word 'theatre' is from the Latin *theatrum*, meaning 'viewing place', and was itself a reminder of an ancient heritage. Some small, neo-classical theatres, that very rich Italian princes had built in their 'renaissance' courts for private entertainments, were also planned within a circle. Well-educated Elizabethans who had travelled to Italy would know all about the classical origins of the round Globe, and some would have studied the recently published books on classical architecture by the Roman, Vitruvius, and the Italian, Leon Battista Alberti. These well-illustrated books were available in Latin, Italian and French.

So the Globe was not only a permanent, wooden-framed home for the actors and their platform stage, but also an adaptation of a tradition of theatre-building in stone and marble that reached right back through Rome to Ancient Greece. It had a far older pedigree than the Gothic churches and elaborate palaces that were the other principal sights of the City of London.

All this sounds very grand, and carefully thought out. But Shakespeare's theatre had to be built in a great hurry. James Burbage's lease for the land on which he had built the Theatre in 1576 had been granted to him for only twenty-one years. That time had run out, and the landlord, Giles Allen, was now trying to include additional clauses in a new lease that would have brought bankruptcy to the theatre company. James's son, Cuthbert, who was now in charge after his father's death, objected to the harsher terms and a row began to develop between the two parties. Allen would not yield to entreaty and prepared to take possession of the building by force.

More bargaining followed and harassments of various kinds, and then Cuthbert Burbage and his family decided on unilateral action. Soon after Christmas 1598, the owners of the Theatre and their theatrical associates started, very stealthily, to dismantle the joints of the wooden structure. Then, on 20 January 1599, at twelve o'clock at night, with the help of John Streete, a master carpenter, they carried all the timbers of the building swiftly across the river under cover of darkness. The well-planned operation, which must have involved twenty or thirty men, took everyone else by surprise, and the removal was completed without mishap. The timbers were now ready for reassembly on a new site, and in a new way. They were the basis of the greatly improved theatre, the Globe.

William Shakespeare was now thirty-five years of age and writing two plays a year for the Chamberlain's Men who performed in Burbage's theatres. His success of the year which saw the opening of the Globe was the comedy *As You Like It*. In Act Two he wrote a speech that seems to allude to his ambitions for the theatre:

> All the world's a stage;
> And all the men and women merely players;
> They have their exits and their entrances,
> And one man in his time plays many parts . . .

Perhaps it was Shakespeare who had thought of the name for the new theatre: its stage will show the world, to the world.

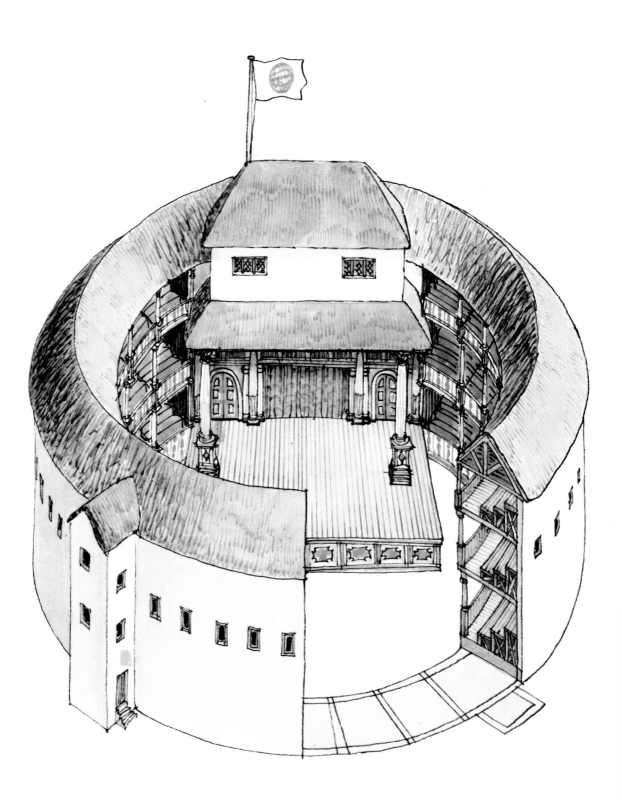

The Interior

When a new theatre is built today there is always keen competition between architects for the job of designing it. The building has to provide for two essential and very different functions: the actors must have a territory in which to perform, and the audience must be able to get a good view of the actors and be able to hear everything. Finding a dynamic relationship between stage and auditorium is a fascinating task which every age has solved in its own way.

The basic plan of the Globe was simple and bold. A rectangular acting area was placed on a wide chord of a circle so that it extended out to its centre. This stage was a platform raised about five foot above the level of the circular 'yard' in which some of the audience would stand to see the play. This central area was open to the sky, except immediately above the stage which had its own roof supported on two pillars. The circular structure around the yard housed three galleries, one above the other. These were open on the inside and furnished with seats in two, three or four rows on rising steps. The galleries were held up by pillars, so that if you sat in one of the rear seats you might have to bend sideways to see everything on the stage.

In this circular theatre the natural place to look was the centre front of the platform stage. Here an actor could command the attention of everybody. John Webster, a dramatist ten or more years younger than Shakespeare, put it like this:

> Sit in a full theatre, and you will think you see so many lines drawn from the circumference of so many ears, whiles the actor is the centre.

The Globe, like any good theatre, was an exciting place to enter. You would walk up to the outside walls which were more than thirty foot high (over nine metres) with only a few, small windows, except in two turrets that protruded a little to give space for stairways to the three galleries. Near each stairway was a small door opening onto a narrow hall-way leading through the lowest gallery and into the yard. It was here that the 'doorman' took your penny for admission. More doormen were stationed at the entry to the gallery stairs to take one or two pennies more should you wish to sit and watch the play in greater comfort. If you sat in the first or second gallery you would be on eye-level with the actors or a little above them. If you paid still more to sit in a private box (or 'lord's room') near the back of the platform stage you would be so close that you could almost touch the performers.

The business of entering the narrow doorway and finding the best available place would take a good deal of time for there was no regular system of reserved seats. People came an hour or more before the performance was due to begin – we know that the Boar's Head Theatre always closed its doors to casual visitors three hours before a play started – and then they met their friends and drank ale and ate nuts, fruit and other snacks, all of which were sold before and during performances. Going to the theatre must have meant taking a holiday from the ordinary business of life; it could take more than half of a day's working hours.

Everything took place in the daylight, in and around the wide and open yard, so that the audience was able to see and enjoy itself as well as the play. In twentieth-century terms it might be said that the auditorium acted as the foyer as well: the audience was given such freedom to move around, talk, eat and drink, even during the performance of a play, that there was no need for intervals as we know them today. Thomas Dekker, another playwright of a younger generation than Shakespeare, used to say that an audience was like a great beast which the actors, with the dramatist's help, had to tame into silence and attention. On another occasion he said that an audience could behave like a crowd of roaring 'fishwives'.

Suppose, for a moment, that you are the first member of the audience to enter. A silk flag is flying high over the outer walls as a sign that the actors will perform a play today. You lose sight of that as you pass through the narrow entrance door and passage, but then your eyes are caught by a sudden splendour rising up all around you. The thirty or more pillars supporting the galleries and their roof are painted in bright colours imitating the marble and gold of renaissance palaces. (Elaborate church monuments of the period, that survive today in some older churches, show the same effect in much smaller scale.) Two tall pillars support the roof covering the stage; its under-side, called the 'heavens', is painted sky-blue and decorated with shining stars. At the back of the stage are two double doors with windows and balconies above them. Curtains decorated with trees, flowers or life-sized figures hang between the doors and in some windows. Fresh rushes are spread on the stage – customary floor-covering for the halls of great houses. No wonder contemporary writers called the interiors of Elizabethan theatres 'magnificent' and 'gorgeous'. If you had paid only a penny, you would now stand in the yard gazing up at the bright, new-made splendour that surrounds you on all sides and shuts out all sight of the workaday world.

The distance across the yard between the inside edges of the galleries was sixty-five feet or more (about twenty metres), and the stage measured about forty by thirty feet (or around twelve by nine metres). When the theatre was full, two to three thousand spectators thronged around, above and below that stage – a lot of people in a small space. As an actor stepped forward to start a play he was in the middle of more than twice the number of spectators who fill the Olivier Theatre, the largest of the National Theatre's auditoria in London today. Those at the very back of this crowd, at the top of the topmost gallery and furthest from the stage, were little more than fifty feet (or fifteen metres) away. Alone at the centre of the front of stage an actor was the clear target for everyone's attention. The most restless members of his audience were literally standing at his feet in the yard.

Theatre People

The owners of the new theatres in Elizabethan London were property speculators and innkeepers; but James Burbage had two sons, Cuthbert, who was a businessman like his father, and Richard, who became the greatest actor of his generation. When the Globe was built with the timbers of the old Theatre, the Burbages, Cuthbert and Richard, kept half ownership for themselves, but divided the other half between five actors, Shakespeare being one of them. All these actors were members of the Chamberlain's Men, the company who hired the Globe and actually put on the plays, and by this means they had a much closer and more enduring link with the fortunes of the theatre in which they performed than that enjoyed by any of their rivals.

Only one other company had anything like the same public following at this time, and that was the Admiral's Men who played at various theatres owned by Philip Henslowe. Ten years earlier there had been numerous short-lived companies, all struggling for survival. Each was named after a nobleman, for only in this way could actors have a standing above that of 'rogues and vagabonds', which had been the official description of the earlier travelling players, and one which gave them almost no rights in law. But a patron and friend at court was more than a legal necessity and social advantage. The Lord Chamberlain, who protected the company to which Shakespeare belonged, was able to speak for the actors when the Mayor of London and his Court of Aldermen tried to restrict the number of theatre performances so that craftsmen and apprentices should not miss too many working hours in order to go to the theatre.

He intervened when there was danger of play-texts being printed without authorization and thus becoming available to rival companies. On the death of Elizabeth I, the Chamberlain's Men changed patrons and became the King's Men, as befitted the actors who performed most frequently at Court at the monarch's request. The sharers of this company, Shakespeare among them, were each granted four yards of red cloth to make liveries to walk in King James's Coronation procession as 'Gentlemen of the Chamber'.

The Chamberlain's Men was run by eight sharers – in James's reign these were increased to twelve – who nominated one of their number to collect payments. Several times the accounts show that Shakespeare was delegated to do this job. The sharers also planned the repertoire and hired other actors – they were called 'hired men' – and they organized backstage activities, ordered properties and costumes, employed an ensemble of musicians, supervised the storekeepers, and commissioned and purchased new plays. Some of the older sharers tended to specialize in administrative functions, but the players' company was a true cooperative or guild. Elizabethan actors were not hired on an occasional basis by impresario, manager, director or producer, as in theatres today, but they ran their own show.

It was an age of famous actors. The profits of the theatre-boom went to them, rather than to dramatists or even theatre-owners. Edward Alleyn, who was the reigning star before Burbage, bought a country house at Dulwich outside London and was rich enough to found a famous school. Heminges and Condell, Shakespeare's fellows, each became men of ample means, the latter having a country home at Fulham. In his own day, the skill of Burbage was more studiously praised than Shakespeare's: poetic panegyrics were published and elegies written when he died.

But, although the actors became established and famous, their careers were adventurous. Burbage was only twenty-five years old when he first played Richard III, and thirty when he created the role of Hamlet – the actual age of Shakespeare's 'young prince'. At thirty-five he played the very old King Lear. His versatility was remarkable, giving him a far wider range of parts than is customary among actors today.

Quite as famous in the public's eye were the
clowns and fools of each company – in some ways
more so, because each was a personality in his own
right. Books were published in their names and
their distinctive styles and appearances showed
through any role that they were given. Clowns
were renowned for making up their own gags and
adding them to the text received from the playwright. Tarleton of the Queen's Men was the first
and greatest. His face alone, peeping from behind
a curtain, could set an audience laughing, and he
always used his own jester's clothes and carried
drum and fife to accompany his comic songs and
dances. Such sure-fire effects guaranteed success
and, no matter how serious the theme of an
Elizabethan play, there was nearly always an effec-
tive role for the company's chief clown somewhere
in the action. When Tarleton's reign was finished,
he was succeeded in popular favour first by
William Kempe and then by Robert Armin, of the
Chamberlain's and King's Men. These were actors
whose faces we still know from contemporary
illustrations. They had their own costumes, too,
like the long frock-like coat of Armin who specialized in 'natural fools', strange child-like men who
had been born idiots and so were dressed as if they
were five-year-olds.

Compared with today, the oddest thing about Elizabethan actors' companies was that they were all male. Female roles were played by boys – as they were called, although the best of them continued to play women's roles until well past their teens and into their twenties. Elaborate Elizabethan and Jacobean dresses made the disguise of a young man's bodily shape much more plausible than modern dress, and so did the formal manners of the age. Moreover dramatists did not write scenes depending on physical intimacy between the sexes: in history plays and tragedies most encounters are in public places, or when danger, misunderstandings or disguise lessen the need to show close contact or direct sexual feeling; in comedies, elements of pretence, masquerade and play keep minds and talk too active and quick-moving for highly sensual responses. Shakespeare's plays are as much about man's sexual nature as any modern works but, although many actresses have since triumphed in his female roles, all this was conveyed in his own day by male actors, so powerful was the suggestion of his dramatic writing.

Dick Robinson was one of the most famous interpreters of female roles for the King's Men, and it was said that, for a practical joke, he once posed successfully as a lawyer's wife in real life. Each boy tended to work with one particular leading actor, and so skills were passed on and the female roles more carefully and consistently rehearsed than others.

It is as an actor that Shakespeare's name first occurs in theatrical records in 1592, and he

continued to appear on stage until he was about forty years old. But he was not a famous actor and seems to have specialized in older roles with comparatively few lines and few scenes. The first mention he received in print as an actor was an adverse criticism for thinking that he was able to write plays as well as act in them. Most of the dramatists of that time were young graduates from the universities of Oxford and Cambridge. They had come to London to make their way by writing books, pamphlets, poems and plays, and by translating. The 'Stationers' – both printers and publishers – commanded a new and expanding market in which competition for employment was so keen that writers often had great difficulty in earning a living. Many were imprisoned for debt. They might well resent an 'upstart player' who tried to dress up in the fine 'feathers' of rhetoric and poetry, and so snatch opportunity away from those much better qualified. (A closed shop for writers would have been a natural extension of the rigorous system of apprenticeship by which the city guilds of those days protected their trades from exploitation.) Many early plays were anonymous, but that changed when the 'university wits' started to write for the players and to vie for pre-eminence. Shakespeare had entered into this busy, competitive world. We call him a dramatist, but that word was unknown in England until after the Restoration; so was the word 'playwright'. In his own time, Shakespeare the actor joined the university wits in being called 'author', 'writer' or, most grandly, 'poet'.

When books were available only as very expensive manuscripts, poets had depended for their livelihoods upon the patronage of a prince or powerful noble. They became members of the courtly household, on the level of friends and confidants, and so they were given recourse to books, learned conversation and travel to foreign countries. For a very few poets and scholars this tradition lingered on after the introduction of printing, and Shakespeare was one of those who found a patron of his own. This was the Earl of Southampton, nine and a half years younger than himself. In 1593 and 1594, when the theatres were closed because outbreaks of the plague made large gatherings a health-risk, Shakespeare had time to write two narrative poems, *Venus and Adonis* and *The Rape of Lucrece*, the first a lyrical, comic and heroic love-story, the second a moral tale of rape and suicide in ancient Rome. Both were published with dedications to Southampton, the second being markedly more personal than the first: 'What I have done is yours, what I have is yours.' *Venus and Adonis* was a great success, being reprinted ten times in ten years. A contemporary Cambridge critic remarked that 'the younger sort takes much delight' in it. Some, at least, of Shakespeare's sonnets were also written for Southampton, and possibly the comedy, *Love's Labour's Lost*, which has many allusions to people whom the young Earl would know very well.

Shakespeare was unique among writers for the theatre of his time in being a part-owner of the Globe, an active shareholder in an acting company and, for most of his career, a working actor, too. Moreover, he was a poet with a patron to support and defend him. While others might write or collaborate in ten or more plays in a single year and move from one company to another, or else write only occasionally for the stage, Shakespeare maintained a steady output for his own company throughout some twenty years, completing one or, more often, two plays for each new season that ran from autumn to late spring or early summer.

Plays and Performances

Before a new play was ready for performance much had to be done. First, of course, was the writing, and for Shakespeare we know this meant literary research as well as the pleasures and pains of composition. He consulted many books, some of them very large. If all the books he used for *King Lear*, or one of the history plays, were placed in a pile no one person could carry them without some difficulty.

Once a script was finished, the author's 'fair copy' would be made and sent first to the Actors' Company for their approval. Then it had to go to the censor. No 'matters of state or religion' could be shown on the stage on pain of imprisonment for the author and loss of licence to perform for the actors. The Master of the Queen's (or King's) Revels had to read and approve every word, at the players' expense, before official approval was issued for a new play. Yet even this did not prevent some theatres being closed for performing 'seditious, blasphemous or scandalous' plays, and some dramatists, Ben Jonson among them, suffered periods of imprisonment in consequence. At a time of unrest, when the Earl of Essex was challenging the Queen's authority and armed bands terrorized the streets of London, the Chamberlain's Men were forbidden to perform *Richard the Second*, a play already licensed and performed, because it contains a scene in which a king is compelled to renounce his crown: in 1601, the Queen's counsellors believed that this might encourage her enemies and spark off a revolution. The theatre was taken very seriously by the authorities and was allowed to deal with political issues only if they did not refer too obviously to current affairs or seditious ideas, but were set, safely, in an earlier century or, better still, in ancient Rome or foreign countries.

A large proportion of the people of London provided the audience at the Globe. By the end of the sixteenth century, the city had some 160,000 inhabitants, and the combined capacity of the two theatres then in regular use was not less than 5,000 on each of the six days of a working week. This means that, discounting buildings used only occasionally for plays, if the average playgoer went once a fortnight and the two main theatres were a little more than half full, then one in every four or five Londoners patronized the theatre. When the two playhouses were full, in the middle of a normal week-day, one out of every thirty-two people would be found watching a performance while most of the remainder would be working.

The theatres had their fans who were so keen to see the first performance of a new play that the actors were able to charge double for admission on those occasions. And they had to change the repertoire very frequently to maintain this avid interest. Nearly all sorts of people came. An eye-witness has identified 'tailers, tinkers, cord-wainers, sailors, old men, young men, women, boys, girls and such like' in the audience. When an investigation was made by the authorities, they found 'not only gentlemen and servingmen' among the audience, but also 'lawyers, clerks, country men that had law-cases, ay the Queen's men, knights and, as it was credibly reported, an Earl'.

The Mayor and Aldermen of the City of London tried to limit the number of performances in any one week, so that there was less absenteeism from work. Clergymen who believed that idle and expensive recreation was a sin, denounced the theatre as 'Satan's Synagogue' and the 'Nest of the Devil'. They also did what they could to prohibit performances and exhort the people to attend to their work – and to listen to sermons instead of plays. Theatre-owners retaliated by choosing sites in the suburbs, outside the City's jurisdiction, and the crowds followed them gladly.

Plays were printed, as well as staged, after further scrutiny by official censors. Paperback books, measuring about five by seven-and-a-half inches (or twelve and a half by nineteen centimetres), were sold for sixpennies each. Some authors actively encouraged this double sale of their writings but, in order to prevent rival companies from staging their successes, the actors tried to stop or at least delay publication. Sales could be brisk: Shakespeare's *Richard the Second* and *Richard the Third* each went through five editions between 1597 and 1623. Although many of his plays were first printed after his death, in the complete edition of 1623, and although he took no personal interest in publication, sales of individual plays were so good that Shakespeare was often the best-selling author, topped only by sales of the Bible, prayer books and some official publications.

When a new play had been licensed, the next task was to distribute its parts. Shakespeare, as a sharer in the actors' company, knew very well for whom he was writing, and some of the roles in his plays would cast themselves. Normally Richard Burbage would take the lead; and the survival of their names in printed texts show that some of Shakespeare's manuscripts indicated that Kempe the clown and Cowley, his 'feed', should perform certain parts. Others were written especially for John Sinklo, an exceptionally thin actor in the company.

Other jobs to be done for a new play included the assembly of properties, the swords, purses, lanterns, luggage, carts, tables, chairs, and other physical requirements of the text. Costumes had to be sorted out of stock, or especially made, purchased or adapted, as appropriate. Music for songs might have to be composed and arrangements made for having a fire on stage or a procession with many torches. A date had to be fixed for the first performance. The 'book' had to be marked up with warnings for the actors and properties to be ready and cues for music and sound effects. This copy of the play belonged to the 'book-keeper', who acted as prompter and controlled backstage activity.

The actors were not given copies of the play, but only of the words of their own parts with the briefest of cues from preceding speeches. These 'parts' were taken home to be studied and learned. Joint rehearsals were few, except for the boy-actors with their respective masters. Each character was separately prepared because the mornings allotted to the rehearsals of each play had to be used for arranging movement on and around the stage and for sorting out costume-changes and the provision of properties, as well as tackling the physical problems of fighting, banqueting, dancing, processing and other group activities that were commonly required by the texts. There is some evidence that authors 'instructed' the leading actors individually, but for the most part a play was realised fully only in performance before an audience: then the various characters truly met and, with the encouragement of their audience, the actors discovered what dramatic life and excitement was possible. 'Scenical representation,' wrote George Chapman, a dramatist a few years older than Shakespeare, gives to any history a 'personal and exact life' that adds 'lustre, spirit and apprehension'.

In a way unknown today, the actors and audience held the play's fortunes in their hands. There was no director to take charge and accept responsibility. So far as we can tell from the day-to-day records of the rival Admiral's Men, there was no 'run' or special 'production' of a play at the Globe – neither word was known at the time – but each afternoon a different play would be performed. During the 1594-5 season, the Admiral's Men staged thirty-eight different plays, of which twenty-one were new to the repertoire. In 1596-7, there were thirty-four plays, fourteen of them new. Very occasionally a great success was played twice in one week, but once or twice a month was the usual frequency. Records of the Chamberlain's and King's Men are not so complete, but what has survived suggests a similar way of running the repertory.

'Lustre, spirit and apprehension' would obviously be required to perform this ever-changing programme: the number of words the chief actors had to remember is only the most obvious problem arising from such a demanding schedule. Standard ways of staging various types of scenes must have been developed, to be modified according to the demands of each text and the excitements of any one performance. But how nobly or hurriedly, slowly, loudly, uncertainly or sensitively a hero might die, would always be uncertain. When a play returned to the repertoire after a fortnight's break, the balance of the performances, the relative strength of this character or that, could change almost out of recognition, and in the new enactment the words of the dialogue would surely be re-interpreted. The audience went to see *how* the play was played, as well as what was played – as at football a spectator is interested as much in the quality of the game as in the result.

A trumpeter announced when everything was ready for a performance by three calls from a special position high above the tiring house. People still outside hurried in to find last-minute places and, for a moment, the auditorium was hushed.

Onstage and Backstage

Everyone is able to imagine a world of his own. You can sit at home in a room that is real, among familiar surroundings, and yet forget all this reality. In your own mind you may be on the top of a mountain or in a crowd at a railway station. You can be reliving an adventure or a long, difficult job you once tried to do. You can imagine yourself in a country you have never visited, talking to people you have never met. And this imaginary world can seem more real to you than the fact of your sitting at home, as seen by someone who does not know what is happening inside your head.

Television can also transport us to another reality, as we lose ourselves in the picture on the screen. And so can a play in performance in a theatre today. When we look at the stage we see a living picture, that is very nearly real: here is a real space inhabited by the characters of the play in a real manner. Painted scenery, and steps, doorways, windows, furniture and fittings, together with subtle lighting-effects, recorded sound, the appropriate clothes and, occasionally, real bricks or sand or motor cars, all signal unmistakably where the characters are meant to be. We give our minds to the world of the theatre as created for each particular play. We sit back in the dark and take it all in.

In contrast, Shakespeare's theatre depended much more on the audience's imaginary reality. In the Globe you would not sit in the dark, and nothing separated you from the platform on which the play was in action: the actors could even speak to you, face to face. In that sense theatre was more real, but only in that sense. No one tried to create another world on the stage, a living picture complete in every detail. Only one element of a play was real – the actors. They were the centre of attention. What they said and what they did provided the small seed from which a full and exciting imaginative experience came to life in the minds of the spectators. The actors had some aids – notably words to speak that were splendid, exciting and life-like – but nothing like the specially designed settings, complicated stage-management and electronic equipment of the theatres we know today. The audience created the setting of a play with their own imagination.

Most twentieth-century theatre productions require weeks spent in design and planning, and many days in technical rehearsals to fix all the sound, light, scenery and stage-properties. In Shakespeare's theatre plays were put on the stage, even new plays with large casts, in hours rather than days. That is why the term 'production' was unknown. Our stagecraft is complicated, finely adjusted and expensive, but Shakespeare's used very simple materials that were easy to manipulate. It was possible to achieve marvellous and eloquent effects, and Shakespeare took the characters of his plays to mountain-tops, forests, battlefields, dungeons, palaces and hovels. But only in the minds of the audience did these marvels find their fulfilment. Here is Thomas Heywood, a dramatist born a few years after Shakespeare, writing about stage performances:

> So bewitching a thing is lively and spirited action that it hath power to new mould the hearts of the spectators and fashion them to the shape of any noble and notable attempt.

How did so little do so much? How did a play 'bewitch' an audience?

The key word is 'action'. Everything came from the *act*ors. Most obviously, Shakespeare's plays and those of his contemporaries have many, many words: an Elizabethan text has two, three or four times as many as the average modern play. The actors' first task was to speak clearly and with 'lively and spirited action'. By making the words 'real' for each character, the actors brought them to life on stage and in the minds of every listener. So an extraordinary world could be imagined. In the history play, *King Henry the Fifth*, Shakespeare gave an actor words with which to paint a picture when nothing at all was happening on stage:

Let us. . .
On your imaginary forces work. . .
Think, when we talk of horses, that you see them
Printing their proud hoofs in the receiving earth;
For 'tis your thoughts that now must deck our kings.

Later in the play, this Chorus asks the audience to imagine a fleet at sea with 'silken streamers' and the 'ship-boys' climbing high in the rigging, and then the siege of a city with all the noise and destruction of cannon at point-blank range. 'Still be kind', he asks, 'and eke out – or fill out – our performance with your mind.'

But it was not enough to speak clearly. Words were only a part of the total action of the actors, from which a play sprung into imaginative life. When the prince in Shakespeare's *Hamlet* gave advice to the players who had arrived at his uncle's court, he told them to 'suit the action to the word, the word to the action'. If a play had a soldier in it, the audience, said Thomas Heywood, must 'see a soldier shaped like a soldier, walk, speak, act like a soldier'. Another dramatist of the time, Lording Barry, has an actor say that his fellows must show

39

Things never done, with that true life,
That thoughts and wits should stand at strife
Whether the things now shown be true,
Or whether we ourselves now do
The things we but present.

Richard Burbage, the actor who first created many of Shakespeare's most famous roles, was said to be an excellent actor:

never falling in his part when he had done speaking, but with his looks and gesture, maintaining it still unto the height.

He so 'wholly transformed' himself into a stage character that even backstage he was never himself again until the play was finished and his costume taken off.

The shape of the Globe Theatre and its stage encouraged very active performances. The actors had to keep on the move, for only at the very back of the stage could they face all parts of the audience that surrounded them on three sides. Everywhere else on stage, including its focal centre, they had to turn this way and that to be seen by all spectators, and they had to be very sure that their impersonations and actions were so physically complete that they would express what was necessary to the play from all points of view.

The stage was not like a picture, looked at from one direction, but like an arena, a small ice-skating rink or large boxing-ring. Figures in action gave meaning and excitement to the play: contrasts between the different activity of two groups of people, contrasts of posture, costume, movement, tempo, rhythm, between a large group of characters and one isolated figure, between many people standing without movement on stage and, a moment later, one figure who is restless and uncertain where to look or go. Shakespeare wrote plays that call continuously for varied action on the arena of the platform stage – movements and groupings that give constantly changing interest and suggest extraordinary events. One look at a copy of his *Complete Works* shows you how verbally rich his plays are, how full of eloquent, poetic and lively words. If you set the plays in motion in your mind, with the characters moving on the open-sided platform of the Globe Theatre, you will understand that the plays are visually every bit as rich. Watching a play at the Globe could be as exciting as a game of football, hard-fought in a goal area.

Instead of scenery, in our sense of the word, the background to the stage, where it joined the circled galleries of the theatre, was an arrangement of doors, archways and windows. These were part of a façade, very like the screens that were built across the main entrances inside Elizabethan halls. Most striking to a spectator were two double doors, one at each side of the stage. The two parts of each could open singly or together, to admit one character or many. They could open rapidly or slowly, as each character making an entry dictated. They could be fixed open so that the doorway became an arch. A whole procession could enter through one door, and walk, march, or hurry right round the edges of the stage and off the other side. After twenty characters had entered through one door and taken up positions in relation to each other and the centre of the stage, a single character could make a separate entrance through the same door and slowly move round the edge of the stage to survey his assembled victims. When many

characters left through one door, two or three could stay behind to talk together and leave through the opposite door. Since the doors were at different sides of the stage, they could be used to show opposition and conflict, as leaders of two armies enter simultaneously at either side, bringing their lieutenants, drummers, standard-bearers, prisoners or hostages with them, and then confront each other across the broad platform-stage. A chase – a device that is sometimes more exciting in slow tempo, than in fast – could start at one door and finish at the other, after various encounters with other characters or around tables and thrones, or the two pillars supporting the heavens over the stage.

Besides the doors at either side, a central opening could be used at the rear of the stage. It might represent the entrance to a city, defended by few or many. For *The Tragedy of Coriolanus*, gates were placed in the central opening. In this play, the hero rushes to attack a city and the gates close

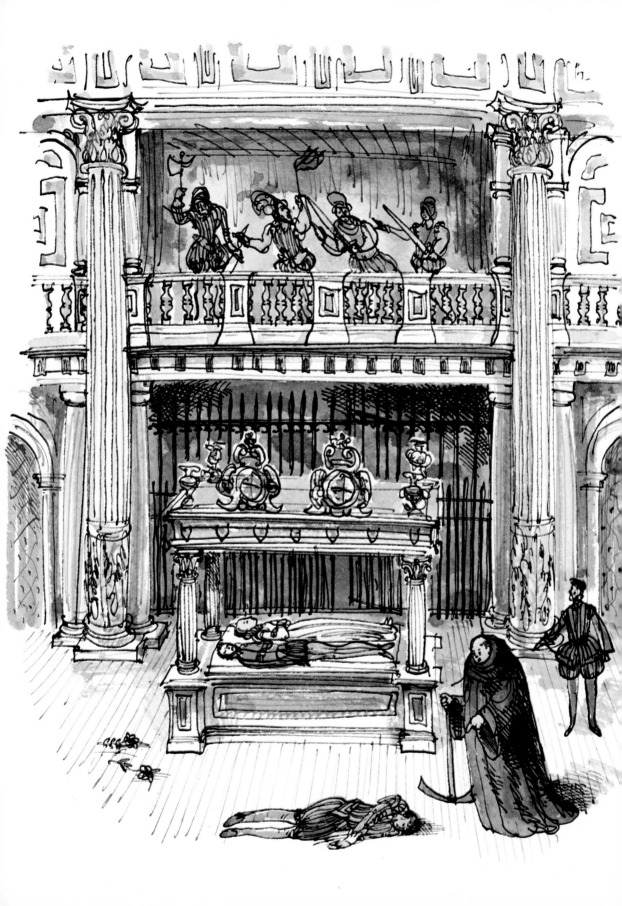

behind him so that the army he is leading is left outside. Later he re-emerges, covered with blood but unconquered; his soldiers take heart and now follow him into the enemy stronghold. So the town is captured before the eyes of the audience. The central opening was also used to represent an inner room, bedroom or study, or a tent. It could be covered with a curtain, and one or two characters hide behind it to spy upon those who are about to enter on the main stage. For the last scene of *Romeo and Juliet*, railings were erected across the central opening and the space behind used as the interior of a tomb. Here a higher level of the rear-stage screen was also used. So the characters first appear above the tomb, and then leave to re-emerge at platform level as if they had descended below ground. The same upper level was used earlier in the play, when Romeo stands on the main stage as if in the garden of Capulet's house, and then looks up to see Juliet at her bedroom window. Sometimes characters appeared on the upper part of the screen, as if on the top of high walls: so the king, in *Richard the Second*, looks down on his enemies from the safety of the battlements of Flint Castle.

The doors and the other openings in the rear screen drew attention away from the centre of the stage and the action was played there chiefly when characters had to be shown as withdrawn from the previous activity. This was especially convenient at the beginning of a new scene, when the characters of the previous scene left through one door and entry through the other signalled a change of location – as from throne-room to bed-chamber or, if the door is left wide open, to battlefield or highway.

Beds and tables could be revealed behind the curtains to present interior scenes, but these properties might also be carried out to centre stage, so that the action is kept closer to the centre of the auditorium and in fullest view. Stage-hands, or 'stage-keepers' as they were called, did this in view of the audience. So the stage-directions of *Macbeth* and *Antony and Cleopatra* call for a banquet to be 'prepared'. In *Coriolanus*, two officers lay down cushions for the senators to sit upon when the stage has to represent a state council. In *King Lear*, stocks are 'brought out' for Kent to be imprisoned and, later, the king is carried in by servants when he is asleep in a 'chair'.

While the Globe did not have scenery, some special stage 'properties' were used to assist the basic activity and to demonstrate the special significance of a particular action or person. Thrones, tables, chairs, stools, beds, altars, coffins, platforms, a grave, a prisoner's bar for a trial-scene, a cauldron and a garden arbour must all be brought on stage for scenes in Shakespeare's plays: in one scene a stage-direction specifies '*low* stools' on which women sit to sew and exchange news of the war. Some properties were used in ceremonies that turned the individual characters into almost identical figures when they kneel, for instance, before a throne as a king is crowned, or as they follow a coffin, all dressed in black.

One of the rare documents surviving from the Elizabethan theatres is a list of stage-properties belonging to Philip Henslowe, the manager of the Admiral's Men. This itemizes many of those properties that are needed for staging Shakespeare's plays at the Globe. Other items in Henslowe's possession are not definitely required for Shakespeare's plays, but could have been used: numerous trees, a canopy, a rainbow and a 'cloth of the sun and moon'. These suggest that a stage property could sometimes indicate a special place or time.

Some very simple tricks were also managed. The stage had at least one trap-door, which could indicate a grave or the entrance to a dungeon or to hell. In *The Tragedy of Hamlet*, the dead body of Ophelia, whom the prince had loved, is 'buried' in the hole left by the removal of the trap-door, and her brother leaps into this 'grave' in a passion of grief at her loss. The simple trap-door would be accepted as a grave, especially since a gravedigger has just prepared it in full view of the audience, digging earth out of the hole with a spade and tossing out old bones and skulls that he says have come from earlier burials. This is a good example of the way in which words and a few simple actions, together with stage-properties, were used by Shakespeare to 'locate' the scenes in his plays and 'move' the characters from one situation to another.

The 'heavens' over the stage was fitted with a small crane that could raise or lower a throne. This was the most spectacular entrance that could be made. It was probably used in the comedy, *As You Like It*, where a god, Hymen, suddenly appears at the very end, entering from 'heaven' itself to bless

the lovers who are about to be married. In *Cymbeline*, the descending throne was in the shape of an eagle on which the god could travel. A stage-direction reads:

Jupiter *descends in thunder and lightning, sitting upon an eagle. He throws a thunderbolt. The* Ghosts *fall on their knees.*

47

Fireworks of various kinds were used for battle-scenes, artillery salutes and lightning flashes. For storms, drums provided thunder and wind instruments the howling gales. Cries from off-stage and trumpet calls of various kinds, the sound of galloping horses (easily simulated) and the breaking of timber or other objects could all be used to supplement an impression of battle. *'Alarums and Excursions'*, *'An Alarum afar off'* or *'The noise of battle'* are typical stage-directions from history-plays. In *The Tempest* there is a storm at sea: here a direction says *'The Mariners enter wet'* and there is a great deal of rushing hither and thither and many varied cries as a sound-effect indicates that the ship 'splits'.

Music, provided by the theatre's own musicians playing backstage or, where appropriate, on the stage itself, would sometimes set the mood for a particular moment, expressing joy, loneliness, sorrow, religious solemnity, animal high-spirits or innocent merriment as the play required. Brass or wood instruments are sometimes specified, and also drums and viols. Several special compositions for theatrical use have survived, especially from Jacobean times.

None of these stage devices was used frequently or took attention for long from the centre of the

drama, the actor. So it is appropriate that the most expensive and carefully considered part of Elizabethan stagecraft was concerned very intimately with the performers: this was the costuming of a play.

An acting company's most irreplaceable possessions were its playbooks, because these were the foundation of their repertoire, but its most expensive were the costumes. They were very numerous and were essential for giving appropriate life and clarity to performances. The area behind the stage at the Globe was largely a close-packed wardrobe. It was actually called the 'tiring house', and was in the charge of a 'tiremaster'. Costumes did more than anything, beside author and actor, to define what was happening on stage, who the characters were and how they were related to each other. It was an age in which everyone dressed in a way that showed his function and position in society. Official regulations laid down how much ornamentation different classes of people could wear. The richest in the land showed their rank by wearing cloth made of gold thread with embroidery that displayed hundreds of pearls and other jewels. Thousands of hours would be spent in making a single suit of clothes, using silks brought from the east and velvets from Italy.

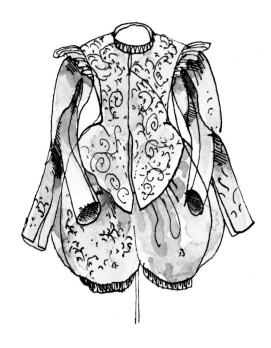

Again the papers that have survived from Philip Henslowe show us the extent of a theatre wardrobe's resources. Among his many cloaks were a scarlet cloak with gold laces and buttons and another with silver trimmings. Others were in satin, velvet, damask, taffeta and a black tufted material. Gowns, suits, jerkins, doublets, french hose, and Venetian breeches were all listed in various cloths and colours, and with many different ornamentations. Some costumes were bought and kept for special appearances as specified by authors of particular plays. One black velvet cloak 'with sleeves embroidered all with silver and gold' cost twenty pounds ten shillings and sixpence – that is 4,926 pennies, perhaps as much as the entire sum collected at a performance at the Globe Theatre, and certainly more than twice the ten pounds which was the normal fee for a private performance at the Court of Elizabeth or James. (In contrast, the work of dramatists was inexpensive; the text of a new play and the right to perform it as often as he wished cost Henslowe a modest five pounds.) At prices like these, it is no wonder that the players used to get some of their costumes second-hand from courtiers who had already shown them off in real life.

All of Shakespeare's plays were performed in modern dress. A special toga for a Roman or an old-fashioned doublet for a king from ancient times were partial exceptions that might be made. Normally the actors were at home in what they wore, even if they represented characters long since dead. The audience saw on stage people they might see in the street, a country lane or a royal procession. Such sights were not dull, because the plays encouraged great variety in dress by shifts of scene, different kinds of activity, and men and women from all ranks of society.

Henry the Fifth is a fair example of this lively visual variety deriving from both costumes and actions. First enters an actor to speak a prologue, with brave words and an eye-catching costume. He leaves and then two clerics, or church-men, busily and warily, get ready for a royal audience, dressed in long robes and mitres as befit the Bishop of Ely and Archbishop of Canterbury. Then the stage fills for the first time, as the young Henry the Fifth sits in state surrounded by older nobles in formal positions according to rank and dignity. Here the full panoply of heraldry would be em-

ployed, expressing to trained eyes the families to
which each character belongs and the functions
they perform at court. The next major change is
the silent entry of the French Ambassador whose
followers carry a present; this procession has no
weapons but is marked by foreign colours. There
is an attentive silence as only one of this new group
speaks. Then the present is displayed – tennis
balls, playthings for the foolish king that the
French believe Henry to be. The king rises in fury
and dismisses the embassy in powerful, energetic,
but firmly controlled words. The Ambassador's
train leaves without reply and only the old Duke
of Exeter dares speak to break the tension. Then
Henry leads everyone off-stage with a call to arms.

Once more an actor enters alone as Chorus, to
be followed not by clerics or royalty, but by two
ragged, blustering soldiers, and then a third who is
accompanied by his wife, an old tavern keeper.
They quarrel with old swords and many oaths
until a boy rushes in, his eyes red and his body
shaking as he tells of someone dying. Now again
royalty enter but the costumes are all quite different now: the army is off to war and ships are
waiting; armour is worn and weapons are no
longer ceremonial. Soldiers march forward to
arrest three men of high treason. Then we see the
same common soldiers in their war gear, followed
quickly by the French Court grouped around an
aged king, and still in ceremonial dress.

After one more appearance of the Chorus, the play takes us to a siege, with scaling ladders outside the city gates of Harfleur: now all is rough, tired and bloodstained, but the king calls out for renewed attack and tiger-like action. A battle cry rings out, and everyone rushes from the stage while the cannon blast away, shaking the timber structure of the theatre.

Many other changes of spectacle follow: a parley with the citizens on the walls of the besieged city; a calm moment for two women at an English-language lesson in a French palace, their clothes informal, flowing and soft, and their voices almost wholly gentle. From now on, until the last scene, the king is seen dressed for battle, except in one meditative episode when he walks among his half-sleeping soldiers at night, his royal insignia hidden by a cloak so that he is taken for an ordinary man. Because this is a night-scene played in the day-light conditions of the Globe, acted tiredness and torches or other lights are used to set the scene.

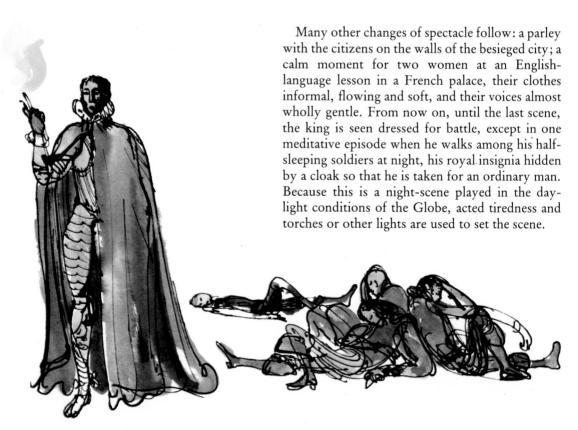

The play concludes with a formal scene in which the English '*enter at one door*' and the French at '*another*' on the opposite side of the stage. It is peace once more: weapons are no longer at the ready and soldiers no longer in attendance. A formality of a new, more intimate and peaceful kind is established as the English King and French Princess are engaged to marry in a public ceremony. The old enemies mingle together as they move off-stage with accompanying music of changed mood. So the play ends on a gentle upbeat, until the Chorus enters once more to warn that the peace will be broken on Henry's death and to beg for the audience's applause. The last spectacle of this crowded play is an actor alone on an empty stage, in contemporary dress as every character has been. He bows to his audience: in their minds, the play will continue to live.

In moments between performing, the actors have been busy backstage, changing costumes according to the needs of each scene, applying and wiping off the blood, lighting and extinguishing torches, finding appropriate properties such as crowns and sceptres, French or English, swords and other weapons – old, new, bloody or ceremonial. Some have had to find purses, gloves, tennis balls and other small articles; one needed a leek that has to be eaten each time the play is performed. They have been helped by the 'tire-men', and by 'stagekeepers' who have got thrones at the ready and, perhaps, camp-fires and cannon. These backstage men have also fired the cannon and given cues to musicians. On stage the actors have held attention as they spoke and moved. The spectacle has been continuously alive as they have changed their costumes and suited their actions to the demands of the words.

Private Theatres

Although all Shakespeare's best-known plays were performed at the Globe and many of them were written especially for that theatre, they were also performed elsewhere, in the halls of great houses, and college halls at the universities, and at Court. These were private performances, paid for by the monarch's Master of Revels, the Fellows of a College or a lord who wished to entertain very special guests. In February 1602, for example, the lawyers of the Middle Temple in London hired the Chamberlain's Men to perform *Twelfth Night* at their 'feast'. We know that one of Shakespeare's last plays, *The Tempest*, started off the winter season of court festivities in 1611. The King made a point of attending a play each Hallowmas, or All Saints' Day, and on this occasion we happen to know that James Maxwell, Gentleman Usher in charge of the Banqueting Hall at Whitehall, had employed nine assistants for six days preparing for this performance and two others in the same week, all by the King's Men. This hall provided a space much the same as the auditorium of the Globe, but in the shape of a 'long square'. It was fitted out with a stage at one end and seats in tiers, some of them in a gallery with small enclosures or boxes.

Here is the Venetian Ambassador's account of attending a performance of a masque – a short but lavish entertainment, both dance and drama – a few years later:

The Banquetting Hall is fitted up like a theatre, with well-secured boxes all round. The stage is at one end and his Majesty's chair in front under an ample canopy. Near him are stools for the foreign ambassadors ... Whilst waiting for the King we amused ourselves by admiring the decorations and beauty of the house with its two orders of columns ... The whole is of wood, including even the shafts, which are carved and gilt with much skill. From the roof of these hang festoons and angels in relief with two rows of lights ... Although they profess only to admit the favoured ones who are invited, yet every box was filled, notably with most noble and richly arrayed ladies, in number some six hundred and more according to the general estimate. On the King entering the house, the cornets and trumpets to the number of fifteen or twenty began to play very well a sort of recitative.

The Tempest was most suitable for such an occasion. It has many dances and decorative characters, like goddesses, water nymphs, 'sunburnt sickle-men', yelping hounds in full chase, a harpy (half-woman, half-bird) and an unspecified number of 'strange shapes' that dance *'with gentle actions of salutations'*. The Queen of Heaven, Juno, *'descends'* in a chariot which would utilize the flying device with which the banqueting hall was equipped. After the short but spectacular first scene of a shipwreck, all the action takes place on a rural island, so that the players might have utilized painted scenery that had been prepared for an earlier court masque. Certainly the candle-light, the enclosed theatre and the high-ranking audience would have been very appropriate to this play about enchantment, court politics and the betrothal of a prince and princess.

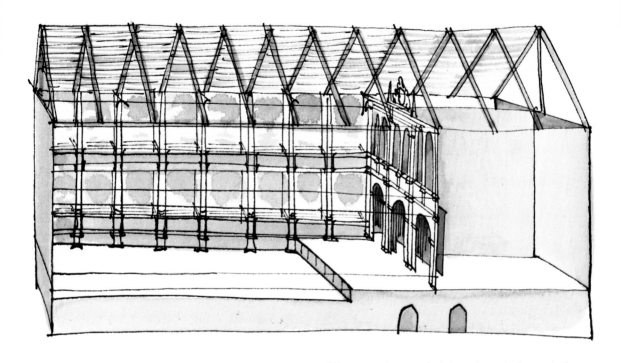

The experience of giving these indoor performances before very special audiences may have
prompted James Burbage, back in 1596, to buy the
hall of a former Priory in London, called the
Blackfriars, and set about turning it into what was
called a 'private' theatre, with a stage a little
smaller than the Globe's and with seats in the body
of the auditorium and two galleries. The land on
which this hall stood was, by reason of ancient
rights, outside the control of the City Aldermen
and so the Blackfriars offered a place to perform in
bad weather to which the audience could come
without travelling to the suburbs – an advantage
that would be doubly welcome when the Globe
was built south of the River Thames. But Burbage
did not live to see the Blackfriars in use because the
local residents organized a protest to the Privy
Council about the crowds that it would attract and
especially the 'vagrant and lewd persons' that
attended theatres. They went on to argue that the
'noise of drums and trumpets' would disturb ser-
vices in the local church. For the time being, the
guardians of respectability had their way, but
permission was given subsequently for a company
of boy actors to perform there. When they went
out of business in 1609, Burbage's sons applied
again and, although the City by now had established control over the precinct, this time they
were successful.

Burbage constructed his theatre in the upper storey of a building with inside measurements of 100 by 46 feet (30 by 14 metres). Only 66 feet (a little over 20 metres) of its length was used – 12 feet (just over 3½ metres) shorter than a lawn-tennis court – and, as at Whitehall, a raised stage was set at one end, about 29 feet (8.8 metres) wide by a little less than 20 feet (6 metres) deep. It was backed by a tiring house, like those of the public theatres, providing three entrances to the stage and openings at a higher level. It probably had a space of 11 feet (just under 3½ metres) behind its façade. There was a central trap-door and a machine for 'flying' a throne up and down from the roof over the stage. Two galleries for spectators faced and surrounded the stage on three sides. All the audience were seated, and prices for entry started at sixpennies for the galleries, rising to eighteen for the pit or central seats, twenty-four for a seat on the stage itself, and thirty pennies for a box at the side of the stage.

The King's Men could perform the same plays at Blackfriars as at the Globe because its shape and equipment were similar. But there was a real difference in effect. The private auditorium was smaller, seating only one thousand, and there were seats for everyone. The audience was more fashionable and wealthy, and better educated, too. Because the theatre was not open to the sky, it was quieter and had better acoustics.

The King's Men had two new, younger dramatists, John Fletcher and Francis Beaumont, who specialized in plays for the Blackfriars, but Shakespeare, older and near the end of his productive career, devised many new tricks for the new opportunity and higher box-office takings. His last four plays, including *The Tempest*, that were written after the more intimate Blackfriars was opened, are different in style from the others. They all use instrumental music and spectacular entries for gods or apparitions. Speeches are often less outspoken and lively than before, with longer sentences, more careful and elaborate arguments and, at times, greater economy. Sometimes the characters have strange and half-hidden feelings. They are spectacular, sophisticated and mysterious plays, and their audiences must have talked about them a great deal afterwards.

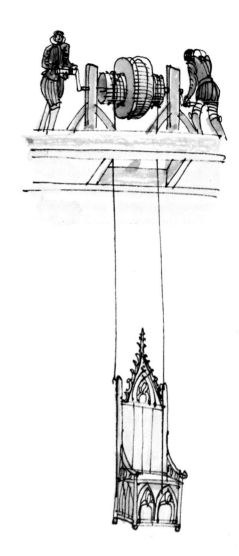

The Theatre Rebuilt

The Globe Theatre was built in a great hurry, in the middle of the theatre season. It was destroyed even more quickly. On 29 June 1613, during a performance of Shakespeare's *King Henry VIII*, a cannon was shot off as a sound effect to accompany an entrance of the King. A spark caught the thatched roof and flames broke out that were carried by the wind. The theatre had to be evacuated through its two narrow doors and within two hours everything except the foundations was a smoking ruin.

Rebuilding on the old foundations started at once, but 'in far fairer manner than before' and with some modifications. More space that could be used for storage of costumes and smaller properties was provided above the stage. A new superstructure covered over almost half the yard, and it may have been self-supporting, so that there was no longer need for the two pillars that used to support the 'heavens'. In less than a year the second Globe was open and was a great success. It was rumoured that King James and certain noblemen had helped towards its cost, but none of the documents surviving show any trace of such a subsidy.

Two years after the rebuilding, in 1616, William Shakespeare died at New Place, the home that he had bought near the centre of Stratford-upon-Avon, the small Midlands town where he was born and grew up. But a few years later, Ben Jonson, a younger poet whom Shakespeare had helped at the beginning of his career, wrote a poem in his memory and claimed that Shakespeare was still alive in the dialogue that he had written for his characters: he was a poet 'not of an age, but for all time'. The prophecy has been proved to be no exaggeration.

In 1644, Sir Mathew Brand pulled the Globe Theatre to the ground to build tenements in its place and in the Great Fire of London any foundation or other relic that might have been left was utterly destroyed. But Shakespeare's theatre, like his plays, lives on in other forms. During the Commonwealth performances were banned by the

government, and yet immediately afterwards two London theatres vied with each other in presenting the plays. Since then there has always been a theatre for Shakespeare, sometimes not much like his own Globe, but still able to bring the plays to life in new styles, with new actors and actresses, and for new audiences. In the twentieth century a number of theatres have been built in imitation of the Globe and at the same time radio, film and television have provided entirely new conditions for performance and enjoyment.

Today Shakespeare's theatre takes many forms, but the plays were written for the original Globe and Shakespeare worked with its managers, actors, stagehands, book-keepers and tiremen, and entertained its crowded audiences. The more we understand of Shakespeare's own theatre and its way of working, the better we shall enjoy and appreciate the vitality of the plays.

Artist's Note

The drawings have been derived from contemporary sources. The exact shape of the Globe has been for long a matter of conjecture; ideas about its appearance differed widely due partly to reliance on now devalued contemporary illustration. The Globe reconstructions shown here are the result of the present consensus of scholarly opinion about the nature of the original Globe. Any Shakespearian student owes a debt to the visual realisations of C Walter Hodges. The portrait of Shakespeare is based on an engraving done after his death by Martin Droeshout. It is the only reasonable likeness to which we have access and was authenticated by its publication in the first collected edition of the plays in 1623.